Hello, Mommy

ZooBorns!

by Andrew Bleiman and Chris Eastland

The photos in this book were previously published in
ZooBorns: The Newest, Cutest Animals from the World's Zoos and Aquariums.

Ready-to-Read

Simon Spotlight
New York   London   Toronto   Sydney   New Delhi

SIMON SPOTLIGHT
An imprint of Simon & Schuster Children's Publishing Division
1230 Avenue of the Americas, New York, New York 10020
Text copyright © 2013 by ZooBorns LLC
Photos copyright © 2010 by ZooBorns LLC
The photos in this book were previously published in *ZooBorns: The Newest, Cutest Animals from the World's Zoos and Aquariums.*
All rights reserved, including the right of reproduction in whole or in part in any form.
SIMON SPOTLIGHT, READY-TO-READ, and colophon are registered trademarks of Simon & Schuster, Inc.
For information about special discounts for bulk purchases, please contact Simon & Schuster Special Sales at
1-866-506-1949 or business@simonandschuster.com.
The Simon & Schuster Speakers Bureau can bring authors to your live event. For more information or to book an
event contact the Simon & Schuster Speakers Bureau at 1-866-248-3049 or visit our website at
www.simonspeakers.com.
Manufactured in the United States of America 0822 LAK
10 9 8
Library of Congress Cataloging-in-Publication Data
Bleiman, Andrew.
Hello, Mommy ZooBorns! / by Andrew Bleiman and Chris Eastland.
p. cm. — (Ready-to-read)
ISBN 978-1-4424-4383-9 (pbk. : alk. paper) — ISBN 978-1-4424-4382-2 (hardcover : alk. paper) —
ISBN 978-1-4424-4384-6 (ebook) 1. Zoo animals—Infancy—Juvenile literature. 2. Parental behavior in animals—
Juvenile literature. I. Eastland, Chris. II. Title.
QL77.5.B5384 2013
591.3'92073—dc23
2012020354

Welcome to the wonderful world of
ZooBorns!

The newborn animals featured in this book live
in zoos around the world. Get to know them through
adorable photos and fun facts written in language that
is just right for emerging readers. Your child might not
be able to pronounce all the animal species names yet,
but if you stay close by, you can help sound them out.

This book can also be used as a tool to begin a
conversation about endangered species. The more
we learn about animals in zoos, the more we can do
to protect animals in the wild. Please visit your
local accredited zoo or aquarium to learn more!

Baby flamingo is hungry. Mommy flamingo is there to give her baby something to eat.

Hello, mommy flamingo!

Stay close to mommy,
baby zebra!
A baby Grevy's zebra can
run along with the herd
when it is only an hour old.

Hello, mommy zebra!

Hang tight, baby tamandua!
Northern tamanduas
are anteaters.
A grown-up tamandua
can eat 9,000 ants in a day!

Hello, mommy tamandua!

These furry cuties are
Vancouver Island marmots.
They touch noses to say hi.
Can you touch noses with
someone you love?

Hello, mommy marmot!

This mommy swift fox watches over her babies. Swift foxes are small . . . as small as house cats!

Hello, mommy swift fox!

Margaret, the baby giraffe,
is giving her mommy a kiss!
Margaret and her mommy love
to be close to each other.

Hello, mommy giraffe!

This baby white rhinoceros weighed 100 pounds at birth. That is a big baby! Someday she will be as big as her mommy.

Hello, mommy rhinoceros!

This mommy western lowland gorilla adopted this baby as her own!

His name is Hasani.

They love to play!

Hello, mommy gorilla!

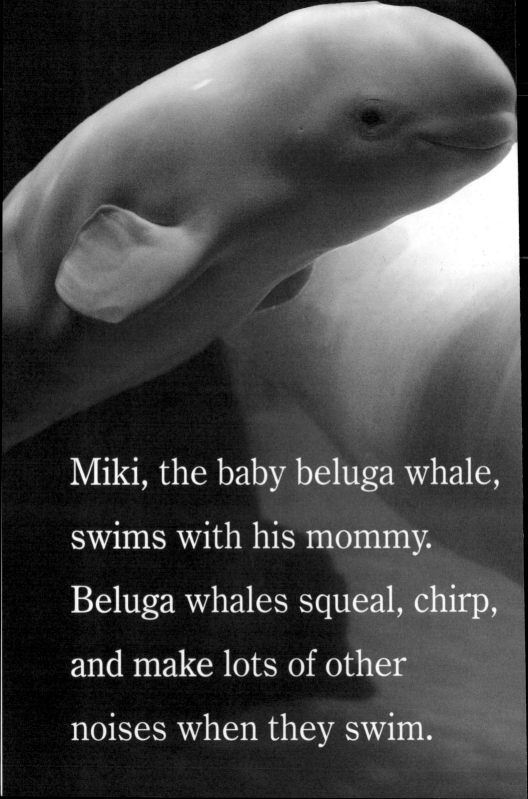

Miki, the baby beluga whale, swims with his mommy. Beluga whales squeal, chirp, and make lots of other noises when they swim.

Hello, mommy beluga whale!

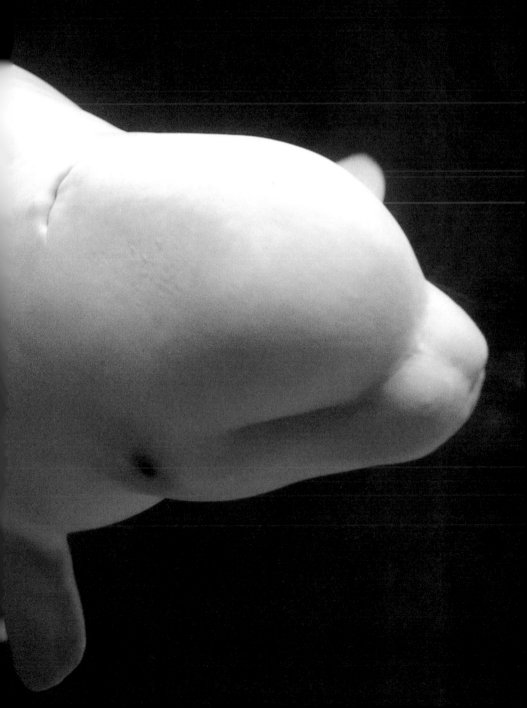

Willie, the mommy chimpanzee, carries her baby wherever she goes. At night, she builds a nest in a tree where they sleep.

Hello, mommy chimpanzee!

Special thanks to the photographers and institutions that made ZooBorns! possible:

AMERICAN FLAMINGO
Ron Brasington/Riverbanks Zoo and Garden

GREVY'S ZEBRA
Matt Marriott/Busch Gardens, Tampa Bay

NORTHERN TAMANDUA
Jason Collier/Discovery Cove

VANCOUVER ISLAND MARMOT
John Ternan/Calgary Zoo

SWIFT FOX
Jennifer Potter/Calgary Zoo

GIRAFFE
Margaret Abigail
Julie Larsen Maher © WCS/WCS's Bronx Zoo

WHITE RHINOCEROS
Matt Marriott/Busch Gardens, Tampa Bay

WESTERN LOWLAND GORILLA
Bawang and Hasani
Marianne Hale/San Francisco Zoo

BELUGA WHALE
Miki
Brenna Hernandez/© Shedd Aquarium

CHIMPANZEE
Willie and Wingu
A.J. Haverkamp/Dierenpark Amersfoort